Beyond the Back of the Bus

Miss Rosa Parks and the Civil Rights Movement

Sandra Turner-Barnes

Illustrated by Bernard Collins Jr.

TWP
Third World Press
Progressive Black Publishing Since 1967

Chicago

Third World Press
Publishers since 1967
Chicago

First Edition
Printed in the United States of America

Library of Congress Control Number: 2010925073

ISBN 13: 978-0-88378-294-1 Cloth edition
ISBN 13: 978-0-88378-295-8 Paper edition

14 13 12 11 10   6 5 4 3 2 1

This book is dedicated to all of my children,
My daughters, Richelle & Renelle
And my grandchildren,
Reggie, Richone, Mia & Journee
And
To any and all future grands or great-grands—
MomMom truly loves you!

This book is dedicated to the memory of
My mother, Betty,
And an entire generation of ancestors
Who lived and died in this imperfect world,
Trying to make it better.
This book is also dedicated to my brother, my sisters,
My father, Boot, and to all my precious family and friends,
I love and appreciate you all.

This book is especially dedicated to the memory of
Miss Rosa Parks and Dr. Martin Luther King Jr.
And to each and every individual, Black, White and other,
Who suffered, survived, and/or died as a victim of Civil and Human
Rights violations, that shameless period in American History
This book is meant to provide encouragement and hope
that God will help prevent these injustices
from ever repeating themselves!

And finally, with sincere love and devotion,
This book is dedicated to all the children of this world,
May God bless you with His Grace and strength, for
Someday, It may be your task to correcct the past.

"Let each of you look not to your own interests, but to the interests of others."
Philipians 2:4

Listen, can you hear the ancestors?
They are whispering Miss Rosa Parks' name,

Still bragging on her great contributions,
So proud of the "shero" she became.

Can you imagine the ancestor angels
Welcoming Miss Rosa to the throne?

Congratulating her for the work she has done,
Showing her the comforts of her heavenly home?

Angelic family and friends, already there,
Were surely happy to greet her.

Martin, himself stood by her chair,
Said it would be his pleasure to seat her.

Miss Rosa Parks was wondrous and wise.
She was chosen by God to do what was just.

She was selected to somehow help find a way
To move us beyond the back of the bus.

History tells us her life
had not been easy and
How Southern Blacks suffered
much distress and pain.

They were cruelly persecuted
and denied civil rights,
Some were attacked abused and
treated as less than human.

Her story began in Montgomery, Alabama in 1955
After another ordinary day,

Miss Rosa was riding the bus home from work
Until Jim Crow jumped in her way.

Now Miss Rosa just wanted to have a restful ride
Found a "Colored Only" seat where she sat,

Had not planned anything special that night,
But suddenly, the past and the future met.

Even though, Miss Rosa had already paid,
She got off, and climbed on again in the back,

Forced to sit behind the eleventh row
Of the bus in a seat designated for Blacks.

But you see, Miss Rosa was wondrous and wise,
Determined to do all the things she must,

Yet, indignity and hate stared her right in the face
As she sat on the back of that bus!

The bus driver firmly told her to move,
To give her seat to a man who was White.

Told Miss Rosa to move or she would go to jail.
Well, she kept her seat and went to prison that night.

This quiet, gentle act of defiance
Encouraged others to take a stand.

This was the beginning of the end of segregation.
That is how the Montgomery Bus Boycott began.

Miss Rosa's courage became contagious,
Not one Black person dared to ride.

For a year and four days,
fifty thousand people walked,
United together
and motivated by pride.

CLEVELAN

2857

Miss Rosa Parks was wondrous and wise,
In God, she placed her trust.

And despite fear and danger,
she took a stand
To help move us
beyond the back of the bus.

Today, struggles continue for people everywhere.
There is so much work for each one to do.

Remember, the ancestor angels watch over us all,
And they are looking for good people like you!

Words to Remember

Ancestors — Individuals who lived and/or died at a period of time.

Angels — Heavenly or spiritual beings.

Jim Crow — A make believe character created by White racist minstrels to portray Blacks as inferior human beings; this name was later sometimes identified by a large black crow, and then used in order to establish and justify cruel and unjust laws and actions against Blacks, including brutal beatings, murders, and lynching, throughout the early 1800s up to the 1960s and beyond.

Montgomery Bus Boycott — Montgomery, Alabama, December, 1955 — following the arrest of Mrs. Rosa Parks for not giving up her "Colored Only" seat to a White man, over 50,000 Blacks boycotted the buses and walked for a year and 4 days. Without Black riders, the bus system faced financial ruin; the boycott demanded that the buses be desegregated, and that African American drivers be hired.

Segregation — White imposed discrimination and separation of Blacks from White society, denying Blacks their legal right to attend the same schools, eat in the same restaurants, use the same toilets, or even ride on the same trains or buses, etc.

Shero — A brave and courageous female; a female hero.

First, I acknowledge my Lord and Savior for
enabling and allowing me to write
Beyond The Back Of The Bus
for, I can do nothing, without Him!

I acknowledge and thank my dear friend,
Dr. Diane Turner, who inspired me to compose a poem
to commemorate Miss Rosa Parks passing in 2006,
Which was the beginning of this lovely little book.

I thank and acknowledge my dear friend, fellow poet, and visual artist,
Mr. Bernard Collins,
Whose beautifully brilliant artwork so graciously brings
Beyond The Back Of The Bus to life.

And finally, I am truly grateful to the great poet and author
Dr. Haki Madhubuti,
Founder of Third World Press
as well as Ms. Gwendolyn Mitchell, Senior Editor, and Ms. Relana Johnson,
Graphic Artist
for this awesome opportunity to touch the world
with my words, in hopes of making the world
a better place for our children!

Many thanks,

Sandra Turner-Barnes

About the Author

Sandra Turner-Barnes is the author of four books of poetry, *Always A Lady, That Sweet Philly Jazz, Too Much Woman an[d] But, Mostly Love.* She is the winner of the 1996 Ebon[y] Magazine Literary Award for Short Fiction. Ms. Turner-Barne[s] co-wrote the Sacred Jazz Suite, "For the Healing of th[e] Nations," along with renowned jazz pianist & composer, Mis[s] Geri Allen. She performed her original poetry in this series c[...] classical jazz and gospel concerts in New Jersey and Atlant[a] Georgia.

Sandra Turner-Barnes is an art administrator as well as a[n] artist. She was appointed Executive Director of the Camde[n] County Cultural and Heritage Commission in May of 200[6]. Ms. Turner-Barnes holds a degree in Business Administratio[n] and Telecommunications Management from Peirce Colleg[e] of Philadelphia. Currently, she is also an adjunct professo[r] in the Rutgers' University Roberto Clemente Humanities Course, and serves on the Board o[f] Directors for the New Jersey State Black Cultural & Heritage Initiative.

About the Illustrator

Bernard Collins Jr. was born and raised in Philadelphia and i[s] now a resident of Lawnside, New Jersey with his daughte[r] Lily, and wife, Tamika. He has a Bachelors degree in paintin[g] from Temple University Tyler school of Art and an MFA from the University of Pennsylvania. He is a participant in th[e] National Arts Program and has exhibited at Art Jaz Gallery[,] The African American Museum in Philadelphia, Octobe[r] Gallery and Community College of Philadelphia. Currentl[y] Mr. Collins teaches painting and drawing at Fleisher Ar[t] Memorial.